Sacred Cornwall

Today I dreamed of Sacred Cornwall
Far away from this dismal place,
To escape back to those weathered tors
and feel the fresh wind on my face.

Visiting places which lift my soul
Every glance reveals exquisite beauty,
I must really go back to Sacred Cornwall
and forget all this senseless duty.

Days detecting the contrast in weather
Wild, rough storms and lashing gales,
The warm sun enhancing joyful living
Swirling mist shielding ancient tales.

Far away from the maddening crowd
Lost in the solitude of an essential moment,
No annoying pointless violent noises
Relieved of the pressures of paying rent.

Today I am back in Sacred Cornwall
For everywhere is paradise it seems,
Striding out across this tranquil place
For now I am truly lost in my dreams.

Introduction

This edition of original photographs and essays depicts an essence of Cornwall, that tends to be submerged under a bombardment of modern life. Within these pages is contained a journey through a land of wonder and beauty, of ancient worship sites, holy wells and strange rock formations, that go back to the inception of human life.

As we journey, we follow the Ley Lines through the Churches dedicated to St Michael. Visit Bodmin Moor, discover the order of the Knights Templar, the Holy Wells, the Religions, the Saints, the Legends. Consider Cornwall as a Sanctuary, enjoy the Festivals. Read about the Legend of King Arthur, of John Wesley, who changed the course of Religion in Cornwall, of Robert Stephen Hawker, a vicar of substance and the possibility of a visit by Jesus the Saviour, to our ancient land. For we are visiting Sacred Cornwall.

Cornwall is, but for a few miles, an island. Its history differs from the rest of England. Many remote villages until recently, where oblivious, by choice, of outside life. Close knit communities resented the intrusion of strangers. For everywhere the countryside is alive with mystical and magical feelings that vibrate down to the soul. Contentment spreads its cloak over the land. The inter stratification of legends, myths and fables, combining with religion, love and the living forces of the earth enhances our lives, as we progress along the path to eternal light.

But our minds need to be open, to be allowed to peruse the path that our inner being decrees. However the continue violation of the earth's resources, by the artificial needs of a modern world that grasps and squeezes the precious riches, until the remaining dust is blown away into the desert of human despair, must be prevented. For we overlook the fact, that we rent space on the earth, our existence is fragile, dictated by a whim of the gods. Should we chance fate by stubbornly ignoring the ways of the earth. Abandoning the ancient customs that stir in our memory, but remain locked away because our modern minds are incapable of change, or to giving, or ready to replace.

Cornwall is different, it is a pulsating land of legend and superstition, for sometimes on visiting a crumbling ruin or even a seemingly ordinary church, there is something else. A feeling of contentment, that can surprise the visitor, the area becomes hazy, it draws you in, until you are part of it. It is difficult to describe the sensation, there is a tendency to stumble over the words in the search for the answer, but there is no mistaking its existence.

Cornwall is the gateway to the pursuit of these spiritual goals, somewhere in the county will be a sacred place that will stir the soul of the receptive visitor. A sanctuary for the weary traveller, a resting place for the troubled mind, a tranquil moment to escape the noise and the relentless grasping of the modern world.

Somewhere in these pages the reader may be drawn to such a place, and then they will understand, that indeed, Cornwall is sacred.

Mystic Cornwall

The word mystic can be a difficult word to use, it can have a magical element, which suggests something unreal. There may be an ingredient of mystery which means something to solve. In connection with Cornwall, it seems to point to our heritage, our roots and the ways of the ancient ones, although inevitably there is the inexplicable presence of magic and mystery.

In the everyday hum-drum of life, where our minds have become clouded with prejudices, anxieties, greed and a readiness to achieve irrelavant goals. We seemed to have squandered the gifts of nature, we need to open our senses to the beauty surrounding us, and to find a moment for peace and contentment.

As the concrete jungle of the modern world relentlessly encroaches God's legacy, so Cornwall is fast becoming one of nature's last outpost, a place to lose yourself in its wild beauty, its secrets and serenity. Everywhere you glance, there are ancient stones, holy wells and places of worship. The problem is, what purpose do they serve? Our modern minds seem to skirt around the answers, unable to grasp the facts, treating them as fiction.

However if we draw on the records, legends and fables that go back, way back, to the dawn of human endeavour, we find a time when gods or super-humans lived with the people. They showed the people, the secrets of the world, built the temples and observed the cosmos.

The existence of these demigods have been documented many times, from many countries, for their existence to be easily dismissed. Where these people appeared from or indeed where they disappeared to, is outside the purpose of this work to speculate. However the temples, special rock formations and shrines would appear to pay witness to their existence.

From what we can conclude from ancient documents and customs, an intrinsic plan

was formulated, which accepted that the earth was alive, and combines its elements, magnetic forces and strategically placed structures to harmonise with the celestial bodies producing mystical attributes that is mostly beyond our modern comprehension.

Some, like the virtues of healing and growing are within our grasp, others like the astral plane, reincarnation and spiritual vision, twist and turn within the confine of our minds, we either accept the concept as reality or dismiss them as fables. While others totally elude our senses and remain for the time, tantalisingly out of reach.

As time marched inevitable on, new concepts and cultures were exchanged between different races by travellers and invaders. The arrival of the Celts, bought a period of war and hostilities, although their pagan worship retained the essence of the old ways. Their priests, the Druids, were able to harness great powers. It was the advent of Christianity that saw a battle of supremacy between the worship of God or of the Devil. The early saints converted the people to Christianity, and in some cases, they used holy water and the altar to transform former places of pagan worship to Churches. This intensified the force and power of the site, because of its history of worship.

So the old ways became watered down, the absence of any records, just the passing down by word of mouth meant the gradual fading from the memory. Civilisation influenced by industrialisation and the suffocating righteousness of the narrow minded Victorians left the ancient life behind. Until at present there is a stirring to return, not to the beginning, but to acknowledge that the earth is indeed alive.

Bodmin Moor

A strong piercing autumn wind bringing the cold bleak promise of winter beats against a high craggy tor, from which the beginnings of a mighty river gushes its way down to the valley, lost in the descending cloak of the night. In the gloom the imagination conjures up shadows of the past, the wind carries the sound of battles of long ago. For here in the heart of the county of Cornwall lies the mysterious and timeless Bodmin Moor. Even modern technology has yet to unravel the secrets and legends that stem from its past.

The first settlers on Bodmin Moor were the Stone Age Man, however it was the Bronze and Iron Age Men who made the first significant change to the environment, by clear-

ing the forest that once covered the moors. The many burial places, monuments and hill forts stand testament to their existence.

The next period of time saw Cornwall's history become exactly opposite to the rest of the country, as the Roman invasion and occupation stopped at the River Tamar. Although they explored the county, there was no permanent attempt to colonise Cornwall, because it was of no interest to them. Another difference was the arrival of Christianity, saints converted the people to their belief, and established holy places and Churches whilst in the rest of England this flame of belief was cruel smothered.

The Dark Ages, a period of time between the Romans and Normans, was a period of war, inhuman conflict and paganism. A time when it was difficult to distinguish between fact and fable, and yet amongst this disorder there arose a legend that became the basis of future works of romance and chivalry, of battles between good and evil. An order of life that has even influenced the present day. King Arthur and the Round Table, a King who is probably the most illustrious of them all and yet some doubt whether he actually existed.

The Normans were great builders, and their architecture is still in evidence today. To police the county, many castles were constructed, whilst others were strengthened. Monasteries and Churches were built to a standard, far superior to any seen on the moors before.

Life on the moor was very hard, and indeed survival was much the order of the day. Any form of natural wealth was very important to the population in that area, and Bodmin Moor possessed earthly riches of tin. King John established a charter for tin in 1201 to be administered by a designated town, where miners bought their tin to be checked for quality and to be weighed, and an official seal of approval was given. These towns were called Steiner Towns, and were responsible for judicial matters and setting taxes for their miners. Consequently any town that could attract commercial traffic would thrive and prosper, and to gain the position of a Steiner Town was a recipe for success. Liskeard and Lostwithiel were the Stannary Towns closest to Bodmin Moor.

As time marched relentlessly on, Bodmin Moor watched its inhabitants bask in their triumphs, and overcome adversity. There were unsuccessful marches against the monarchy, the Black Death that claimed almost half the population, conflicts over religion, and civil war, and in 1837 a discovery of copper ore in the hills of Caradon, that brought all the hysteria to Cornwall that are usually reserved for a gold rush.

During the mid-eighteenth century, Bodmin Moor witnessed the arrival of a stranger,

who was to change the course of Cornwall's religion as the Celtic Saints had many centuries before. John Wesley visited Cornwall many times and today his Methodist churches can be seen in most of the towns and villages of Cornwall. Two rooms were built into a cottage at Trewint, near Altarnun for him and his fellow preachers which is still preserved for visitors to see.

Today Bodmin Moor is the ideal place for many people to explore and escape the every day pressures of social, domestic and financial burdens. For it accommodates the needs of many forms of different activities, from historian to horse person, from botanist to hiker and from photographer to rock climber.

Sanctuary

Everyone has the power from within, to achieve their earthly goals, however destiny would seem to disagree. There is a tendency to throw up barriers or obstacles to prevent our progress. As though there is safety in our failure.

There is a feeling of our spirit being separate from our body, our spirit yearns to soar, like a bird on high, caught in the swirling air currents, surveying all below. The master of our destiny.

Yet what stops us, breaking through the paper thin obstacles, is it the human dread of life, or the weariness of our human bodies. Somewhere in our minds, there is a contentment, a place we can escape to, to leave all our earthly problems. A place where we can come to terms with ourselves. For no one else can.

Places of wonder where crystal clear water cascading through time etched channels, foliage of all description bordering this ever flowing stream. The wind softly blows away the fears of our generation, and sweet smelling flowers intoxicate our minds with real hope. A winding path trod by countless pilgrims, leads to a timeless place of gentle peace, the lichen covered stones of an ancient well, emulates feelings of tranquillity, the spirit feels free, the body young and strong. For now having rested it is time to return, and breach the walls and battle on.

A View from a Cornish Church

In the interweaving intrinsics of village life stands the Church. Serene, imposing and ultimately at the heart of all that happens. It has been there since time immemorial, shared in the newness of birth, the happiness of marriage, and suffered in the grief of death. A Church may appear to be stark from the outside and yet inside there is a world of serenity and peace. To sit there in meditation and prayer, and watch heavenly sunlight shimmer through blessed stained glass windows, feel the joy of being one with God, is difficult to explain in mere words.

But now even this wonder is being threatened. The modern world is encroaching, nothing seems to stand in its way. Recession, inflation, cash flow, funding, viability, profitability seem to be words that inevitably pull the old values down and replace them with new computer aided concepts. A sparkling age of wonder and modern technology is upon us.

So where does that leave the Church, criticised as being out-of-date, dull and lifeless? Suffering under the financial restrains of the higher order, even its very existence is in doubt.

So does the Church go with the tide, put its name in lights, get the computer to advise on personal problems? Have video and computer games, pin ball machines and sideshows in accessible places? No doubt the effect would be to minimise costs, and turn a deficiency into a profit, all wonderful technical jargon. But I seem to remember reading that Jesus encountered a similar scene in the house of his Father.

I believe the answer to it all is faith. God will show the way. Maybe that is an intangible asset that does not show on the balance sheet, and it is difficult to equate on a cash flow projection, but it is the important factor that gets you through the day. For in the end it will overcome all, and save our place of reverence. Somewhere for us to sit and to contemplate, for faith in God is the ultimate answer.

The Legends

On its surface, Cornwall is beautiful and serene, and has an endearing atmosphere that gives comfort and fortitude. But bubbling beneath the surface, is a world of mystic secrets, countless legends and stories that delve into the spiritual and supernatural world.

For it is generally agreed that every legend has an element of truth, that gives the reader a chance to discover fact from fiction. However after a considerable time of exploration, it can leave you further from the truth, than you were at the beginning of your search.

Cornwall has a timeless element, that supersedes all attempts to alter its existence, for it has an indefinite history that goes back, beyond human memory and writing. To when legends were told by word of mouth. Your imagination looks back to a time, when the sky is radiantly coloured blue, the sun always brilliantly shines, the warm winds are full of the echoes of the secrets of life. The effect of this paradise is to give your spirit strength and keep you on the path to eternal light.

Here time is timeless, and is an obvious basis for legends. Time eventually covers the starkness of disasters and foregoes the need to register any happenings, but gives purpose to life. Until eventually, you realise that modern day goals can be empty and pointless, and they unfortunately can take you down the path to nowhere.

For at the end of the day, you need support, to strengthen you when you are down and out. Love is an enriching way to boost your life. The love of Cornwall gives you purpose, drinking in the stories, the places, the legends, which keeps you from feeling empty and alone.

In Cornwall, the greatest legend exists. A legend that is indelible in the memory, a romantic age of chivalry, of knights in shining armour, performing heroic deeds to gain the favour of beautiful ladies dressed in long flowing gowns. Modern day values seem insufficient and pale before their quests of honour. The island of the legend, Tintagel, has a quality that is difficult to define. Here is the rumoured home of King Arthur and the Round Table.

Breathtaking views, of mighty waves crashing repeatedly, on rugged rocks. The smell of salt water carried by the prevailing wind, intermingled with the sounds of calls from a time gone by. The imagination starts to take over, as inspired by these rare feelings, the visitor glimpses what might have been. The quest for the Holy Grail, intermittent with thoughts of King Arthur, Camelot, Excalibur, Merlin, Guinevere, the Lady of the Lake and Lancelot enrich the best legend yet. Until we view the thought that fact and fiction are difficult to define, but if you could, would we really want to know the truth, for then the greatest legend would be no more.

Whether King Arthur is fact or fiction, or his place of residence fact or fiction, he remains lost behind the mists of time. However during mediaeval time his history was down to oral inscriptions, which remained in the memory. Until the 12th century, a

Welsh monk, Geoffrey of Monmouth wrote of his existence, which he claims was copied from an ancient British written book, which no longer existed. It was left to the Victorian period, for the legend to hit the heart of the population. Writers of the highest standard were deeply involved in the legend of King Arthur, Sir Walter Scott, Charles Dickens and Alfred Lord Tennyson. The latter had been inspired by Robert Stephen Hawker, the eccentric vicar of Morwenstow, famed for his work on "Shall Trelawney die".

The Vicar's parish was remote, wild and weather beaten, but possesses an air of mystic beauty. It was here that Alfred Lord Tennyson visited the Vicar, who was prone to moods of depression, caused by a lack of people in his parish, with motivation and knowledge. However he was totally unique in his ways, and his spiritual visions have left vicars following in his wake, unable to compete or approach his brilliance. They have to accept him as a being, who was one with nature and enrich their lives with his everlasting divine presence in their parish, for if they reject him, they will be doomed to a life of meaningless and morose existence. For he has shown the way along the path to eternal light, and although his work on King Arthur was considered the best, it was the poet that received the acclaim. For Alfred Lord Tennyson used the Vicar's insight to gain his fame, but in the end, he conceded that Robert Stephen Hawker had "beaten me on my own ground".

The Legend of King Arthur has clearly inspired many people, but Cornwall also, holds claim to another superior Legend. For all over the world, there are many towns lost below the waters, submerged by the continuous pounding of the waves, but the most famous legend was the Land of Lyonesse, which stretched from Lands End to the Scilly Isles. Many towns existed here, but in 1099, it fell beneath the sea, victim of an horrific storm. To add to the legend, it is believed that Lands End is a new name, and also sailors have witnessed the towns below the sea, and have even netted parts of buildings. In 1930, a journalist is reported to have been woken by the ringing of a bell, which he was told was the church bells of Lyonesse.

Many giants have lived in Cornwall, Giant Bolster was a bad tempered brute, who committed acts of unnecessary violence, but he fell in love with St Agnes, a lady of serene charm, who asked him to prove his love, by filling a hole in the rocks with his own blood. After he had cut his arm, and the blood poured into the hole, he discovered he wasn't filling it, and he died before he realised it was bottomless and ran into the sea.

The giant, Cormoran of St Michael's Mount, stole cattle and eventually a reward was

offered to kill the villain. Jack the Giant Killer became famous, when he tricked the giant into falling into a pit, and killed him with a pick-axe. Jack boasted his fame and legend when he visited Wales and killed more villains of mighty statue.

Two Cornish legends happened at Dozmary Pool, near Bolventor and Jamacia Inn on Bodmin Moor. The legendary lake is reputed to be bottomless, and is the place where King Arthur's Sword, Excalibur was thrown, on the instructions of the dying King, and caught by a hand, and taken below the surface. While the other legend, is where John Tregagle, the evil disciple of the devil, was sentenced to emptying the lake, with a leaking shell, for all his vicious inhuman crimes.

A romantic legend in Cornwall exists, that effectively filters into your dreams. The area around Zennor can be icy cold and bleak, but through the village runs a bubbling busy stream that can steer you away from a rut of depression, as it meanders its way to the ocean, through Pendower Cove. Long ago, Matthew Trewhele lived in the peaceful village, and through his rare gift attracted many people to the Church, as his superb singing made even the most musically acclaimed visitor listen quietly in admiration. A Lady of exquisite beauty, with eyes that glowed with the warmth of her soul, dressed in a long flowing gown, became part of the adoring audience, discreetly listening from the rear of the sacred Church. Waiting for the opportunity to speak, the lady used her charms to effectively win his love, and together they disappeared into the ocean of the setting sun, never to be seen again.

However years later, fishermen working from their boat in Pendower Cove, were asked by a mermaid to move their anchor, as it was near to damaging her door. They agreed to move it immediately as it was considered unlucky to verbalise with a mermaid. She thanked them, as she needed to be with her husband, Mathey and children. The fishermen telling the happening to the local villagers were all left in total agreement that the mermaid was the lady, who had enticed Matthew away.

Sometimes in a special moment of peaceful tranquillity, the serene cove seems alive, the warm sun's rays dance in twinkling delight, on the white foam of the gentle rhythmic waves that caress the golden sands. The divine beauty draws you in, until you are part of the spiritual haven, then you become aware of the lovers voices, singing in romantic harmony, that echoes through the salty ocean. Love lives for ever.

Of all Cornwall's legends, there exists a legend that is more than life, it transcends your soul into a golden paradise, where you become one with yourself. St Just-in-Roseland has a holy church, that is saturated in benevolent worship, from a time that supersedes the echoes of human memory. This awe-inspiring area has a mystic

atmosphere of exquisite tranquillity and eternal peace. Mere words fail to justify its vision. Having experienced this special place, and spent time in quiet reflection, the legend became a reality. For in a period, when the area was already sacred, before the church existed, and Roseland was almost an island, and traders were able to travel far up the river, the Saviour of Mankind, Jesus visited this area.

His uncle, Joseph of Arimathea was a tin merchant and reputedly traded in the area. The inception that Joseph would bring his nephew to this sacred place lies easy in the mind, for surely the peace that emulates from the serene area justifies the turning of the legend into history. The existence of Jesus, warms the heart and gives purpose to life. His presence in St Just-in-Roseland, is more than mere words can describe, your soul drinks in the excitement, the wonder, the glory. For at the end of the day, your spirit has witnessed things beyond the comprehension of your mind, gradually as time marches on, it will filter through. Leaving you with the indelible memory of Cornwall's Garden of Eden.

St Michael's Ley Line

Through Cornwall exists the famous ley line, dedicated to St Michael, the Christian Arch-angel of Light, responsible for defeating demons and guiding souls through to the after world.

A ley line is an invisible form of energy which interacts with the earth, and was a factor in ancient sacred ceremonies. This alignment linked the earth and cosmos powers for the benefit of the inhabitants of the planet.

To understand the concept of the ley line, is difficult, as it is deeply rooted in the intricate ways of nature, which has existed since the beginning of time. The physical aspect of the earth's existence seems within our understanding, but beneath the surface is a world of wonder, which seems beyond our knowledge. Although in time gone by, there has existed an intellectual source able to harmonise these ways, and the presence of places of worship and prehistorical sites, along the alignment, built in amazing accurate position, bears witness to this assumption.

Today the intensities of these happenings have been watered down, the time lost essence of these mystic ceremonies linger in the shimmering shadows, tantalisingly out of reach. While on the surface, the main priorities in today's world are money,

power and a striving need to have material objects which keep you above the masses.

The rising sun on Mayday, radiantly shines its eternal light down this ancient alignment. From the most easterly point of East Anglia, to Bury St Edmunds, to Glastonbury, to St Michael's Church, Brentor, near Tavistock, before crossing the River Tamar at Horsebridge. The holy light progresses its way through Stoke Climsland Church, skirting Sharp Tor and through the Cheesewring, a place of abundance of ancient stones.

Before passing through Cornwall's most holiest village, St Neot, a religious centre from long, long ago. The symmetrical size of the imposing church, seems too immense for the village. The striking attributes of this holy place, is its very fine stained glass windows, one being the second oldest in the country, depicting in pictorial splendour , many interesting anecdotes.

Behind the church in a spacious level meadow, filled with lush green grass and an abundance of colourful wild flowers, is the holy well of St Neot, secluded, serene and timeless. Its existence, a link to the old ways, its presence enhances the magnitude of nature's treasures.

On flows the sacred line, through the Glen Valley, criss-crossing the River Fowey, through Lostwithiel, across the China Clay pits, before quickly arriving at St Michael's Mount, the historical holy island. A sanctuary of years gone by, for pilgrims to visit and delve deep into the existence of Saints and uplift their spiritual feelings. St Michael's Mount was once, according to legend, high in the middle of an ancient wood, which links it appreciable to the misty romantic tale of Lyonesse.

St Michael's Ley Line eventually leaves Cornwall at Carn Les Boel, with Land's End in the immediate distance. Along this sacred line, which is strewn with places of wonder, and hopefully has left enough ideas for the reader to explore, expand and experience the joy of this ancient way.

Cornish Influences

Having considered the importance of Legends to Cornwall, places of sanctuary and worship, St Michael's Ley Line and the incredible Robert Stephen Hawker. There are other influences that have etched forever, their contribution to fortifying the quality of

Sacred Cornwall.

Knights Templar were responsible for the protection of the pilgrims, who journeyed the old pathways in the holy lands. Founded in Jerusalem in 1112AD, they took a unique vow of poverty and their military order became the basis for others to follow. Their involvement in the Crusades and the romantic notion of them protecting the name of Jesus by the defence of the Holy Grail is surely stimulating to our spirit.

Such was their totally unselfish and remarkable road to helping others, it gained them unique and unfailing trust, which started to encroach on the very existence of the many forms of religion and royal orders. Because their honourable approach was far superior, and left the other establishments trailing in their wake, the only way open to their demise was a course of brutal and atrocious acts of inhuman violence to silence them forever.

Many Templars were burnt at the stake, after being tortured to confess their guilt, for seemingly irrelevant crimes. But such is the way of the world, an order which upheld the virtuousness of chivalry and worship, is deemed to be destroyed by power hungry people, with evil firing from their eyes.

In Cornwall exists a church called Temple on Bodmin Moor. This haven is bestowed with a feeling of holy righteousness, reputedly founded in the 1100s by the Knights Templar. Which after their malicious downfall and carnage, eventually became a Cornish equivalent of Gretna Green, until the mid 1700s, when an Act of Parliament was passed nullifying this loophole. The church then fell into disrepair for more than a century, during which time the roof collapsed and killed a sheltering tramp. It was rebuilt in the mid 1800s on the existing foundations of the Church of the Knights Templars, retaining the original tower and incorporating many features of the old church.

For emanating from the confines of the Church is an intrinsic interweaving of worship and love, a deeply rooted presence of an aura of peaceful tranquillity. The divine sunlight filtering through the sacred window dedicated to St Catherine, descends directly from heaven. This sanctuary of wonder has retained the celestial memory of the Knights Templars and kept them forever in our aspirations and dreams.

John Wesley (1703-1791) was small in stature but big in conviction for Jesus Christ. He travelled many exhausting miles around the British Isles spreading the word, inspiring and converting others. Today it is possible to see Methodist Halls of Worship in almost every hamlet, village and town in Cornwall, over two hundred years since his last visit. John Wesley has been called the Father of Methodism, and he probably

changed the lives of the Cornish more than any other. His motivation was not of a physical nature like power or wealth, but of a spiritual one, passing a message of eternal salvation.

John Wesley had to overcome many conflicts along the path to his heaven, England was at war with France and Spain, and Bonnie Prince Charles was set to cross Hadrian's wall and conquer all that lay before him. Consequently, the Cornish were fearful of spies, and there was trepidation that John Wesley might instigate a Jacobite rising. He faced a murderous mob at Falmouth, but was saved by confronting them with his belief. The Cornish hostilities were damped by the sincerity of John's faith, and so began the roots of Methodism in Cornwall.

On his last visit to Cornwall in 1789, at the age of 86 he was treated as royalty and preached to multitudes, leaving the country he knew his message would perpetuate in this resolute haven. There is no doubt that where John Wesley could have presented himself as the saviour of the age, he was simply the servant of God.

In Cornwall, in the areas of sacred beauty, where lush green moss, a shimmering health enhancing sun, plants of extraordinary splendour and musically exhilarated birds cherish the enchantment. There is to be witnessed the presence of holy churches, sacred wells and stones of intriguing position. But behind the swirling mists of time, enhancing the sacredness, are the Saints. As the old expression states, "There are more Saints in Cornwall than in heaven".

St Michael the Archangel and St Mary the Earth Goddess have churches dedicated to them in Cornwall, while the arrival of the Saints, that infiltrated the earlier regime of the Druids, made the numbers swell. To some of our population, Jesus is the inspiration to their voyage through life, while others consider him a legend, and a few state a non-existence. But there can be no dismissing Jesus's influences on the Saints that travelled to Cornwall spreading his words of faith.

Investigating into the ways of the Saints and their charisma in the remarkable world of Cornwall can stimulate your spirit, as pilgrims discovered in years gone by. Despite attempts by Druids and Christians to extinguish each others existence, lingering stories will forever give life to each path of worship, leaving visitors to journey the road of their choice, which in years gone by could have resulted in pointless death.

For in the world, there should be treks for each to explore, which shouldn't embroil others, but should be for the advancement of the explorer. In Cornwall, there are many locations to discover and leave the visitor in no doubt that Cornwall is indeed very sacred.

Cornish Festivals

In the old days, working in Cornwall, and being a fisherman, miner or farm worker was very difficult, having to work for long periods and under very strenuous conditions. Consequently, the opportunity to attend a Cornish Festival, was a day to escape the everyday work load, and refresh yourself with a fun day intermingled with family and friends.

Within Cornwall there is a magnificent span of Festivals, some go back to pre-Christian times, and certainly the Flora Dance held in Helston at the beginning of May can be hailed as a superb day of celebrating. During the day, Helston is fully decorated with glistening, colourful spring flowers, and the population deeply absorbed in classic dancing through the crowded town. With the glowing sun at its highest pinnacle, the main dance, overwhelmed with the grandeur, witnesses the ladies attired in elegant long flowing gowns and hats of vivid design, with gentlemen of posture in morning dress, the atmosphere is of a joyful and loving nature.

With strains of St Michael the Archangel, St George and the Dragon, the Spanish Armada and Robin Hood within the Flora Dances, the Padstow Obby Oss celebrates on Mayday the return of the summer season, and the fertilising of the dragon energy. In fact, a return to the ancient days, when life was open to natural feelings and it shakes your spirit free of the irrelevant pressures of the modern world. Padstow has valiantly protected the primeval tradition of the swirling dragons that run amok through the excited town, and so present an unique festival for the visitor to witness.

An engineer, who was responsible for impressive inventions was Cornishman Richard Trevithick, who stirred the life of Camborne to extremely high levels during the Industrial Revolution. The last Saturday in April, is an opportunity to be part of the parade of locomotives, bands and dancers, that steam their way to raising vast amounts of money for charities.

Hurling is an old Cornish tradition that used to be an inaugural part of many Cornish villages' festivals, but currently, it is limited to only St Ives and St Columb. A silver coated ball, approximately the size of a tennis ball, goes screaming through the town, with the opposing sides of the town and the village, trying to score goals. The goal posts are set some two miles apart, many shops and houses have to barricade their windows and doors against the likely bombardment. With St Ives' game being more civilised, taking place in February, St Columb's game on Shrove Tuesday has a more physical encounter and captivates a considerable number of spectators.

In June, there has existed for the last seventy five years, a West of England Bandsmen's Festival. Held in the village of Bugle, situated in the middle region of Cornwall, located in the China Clay area, is a programme for followers of Brass Band to attend. The winners parade the village at the end to the rhythmical delight of the captive audience.

Summercourt Fair held in September, is probably the oldest fair in Cornwall, dating back to the 1200s, and is popular today as it was in centuries gone by. The magnitude of items for sale is very impressive, and furnishes the customers with the opportunity to examine, purchase and satisfy their needs.

While in December, there is a stirring rivalry amongst the Cornish villages, adding a new spectrum to the most sacred and celestial parishes in the world. During the year, these spiritual enhancing sanctuaries, are beautified by cherished flowers. In January, the magical appearance of the snowdrop, gives declaration to the advent of spring. In February and sometimes before, the sun like daffodils, brightens the winter days. In April and May, the carpet like change to the winding trails through the woods, sees the bluebells ameliorate the way through. So when the darkness of the winter descends there is a need for brightness to raise the spirits.

Hence the Christmas lights gives a joyful and merry feeling to the communities within the hallowed county. The village of Lelant in Cornwall is close to paradise, the sacred church dedicated to St Euny, the parish's saint, from a time far faraway, has breathtaking picturesque views across the dunes to the sea. A golf club is situated near the dunes, and bordering the golf course runs the railway line from St Erth to St Ives, giving the passengers the best scenic train ride in the country. Lelant's sparkling white Christmas lights, displayed by all contributing buildings, add to the peaceful feeling, emulating from this place of wonder, giving the village, an uniformed spiritual glow.

Near Penzance, is a old fishing village called Mousehole, whose quay, in the depths of winter, is colourfully decorated with glittering Christmas lights, and is a definite place to visit, to celebrate Christmas. With Newlyn and Mevagissey also giving reason for the visitor to applaud their efforts, the winter lights certainly have given a new route to reach higher levels of cohesion between families and friends.

Good festival hunting!

The Reason for Living

Cornwall has the sacred sanctuaries, which are ideal for spending time in private reflection, and considering the way to find the path to eternal light. For the modern world seems to focus on money, power and irrelevant material requisitions. Yet the only thing that is going to happen is death, so the time spent between birth and the inevitable, should be for the benefit of your soul. Increasing your knowledge and your consideration for other beings. For what do you take with you when life comes to an end. Money? Power? Material objects? What do you leave behind? Your memory will linger with your family and friends, but it will be your children and their descendants, maybe unknowing at first, but the aftermath will became a reality, as time goes by, for they will carry your love, hopes and aspirations, through the dimensions of the future.

In Sacred Cornwall, there are glimpses of enchantment, of a heavenly land which is close at hand, but is difficult to define where it is. A land for the soul to rest, before its next journey. A land which is alive and beyond belief, of sheer wonder and amazement. The spirit of nature pulsates beneath your feet. Your dreams of such a place, becomes a reality, when your soul, after leaving this world, is drawn into the total shimmering atmosphere of this paradise. Your appreciation of the Knights Templars' spiritual quest, for helping others, becomes apparent. To protect souls from evil forces, and give them knowledge of this paradise, rides easy on the mind.

For at the end of the day, there is an interweaving source of knowledge, that runs deep in our souls, difficult to find, because of the interference of the modern world. But aligns us to this place of paradise, where we will eventually come to terms with eternity and the meaning of life, and perceive that the sight of this wonder, stems from meditation in locations of tranquillity, which are realistically discovered in Sacred Cornwall.

Special Thanks to:-

The Paul Watts Cornish Picture Library, who have supplied all the images.
Cornish Lithographic Printers for their printing and finishing.
Paul Broadhurst, whose work on The Sun and The Serpent, Tintagel and the
Arthurian Myths and Secret Shrines were the inspiration for this work.

Published by

R & B Enterprise, Trelawney Lodge, Keveral Lane, Seaton, Cornwall PL11 3JJ
Telephone 01503 250673   Fax 01503 250383
Written by Roger Lock. Design by Barbara Lock.
Supportive work by Barbara Davis.

Picture Index

Front Cover: St Michaels Mount; Inside Front Cover: St Agnes; Page 1: Perran
Sands; Page 3: Stowe's Hill, Bodmin Moor; Page 5: Lansallos; Page 7: Nanjizal,
Land's End; Page 9: Between Buttern Hill and Bray Down, Bodmin Moor; Page 11:
Garrow Tor, Bodmin Moor; Page 13: Daymer Bay; Page 15: Minster Church,
Valency Valley; Page 17: Colvannick Tor, Bodmin Moor; Page 19: Golitha Falls;
Page 21: St Just-in-Roseland; Page 23: Brentor Church, Dartmoor; Page 25:
Horsebridge; Page 27: Wheal Owles Mine Ruins, Botallack; Page 29: Great Wood,
Lanhydrock; Page 31: Falmouth; Page 33: Flora Day, Helston; Page 35:
Trelissick Gardens near Feock; Inside Back Cover: Goss Moor; Back Cover:
Lands End.